THE LIBRARY OF FUTURE WEAPONRY™

BATTLEFIELD COMMAND SYSTEMS OF THE FUTURE

Christy Marx

The Rosen Publishing Group, Inc., New York

To my father, who served his country. And to Alexander of Macedon,
who shared with Sun Tzu a true understanding of the nature of war.

Published in 2006 by The Rosen Publishing Group, Inc.
29 East 21st Street, New York, NY 10010

Library of Congress Cataloging-in-Publication Data

Marx, Christy.
Battlefield command systems of the future / Christy Marx.—1st ed.
    p. cm.—(The library of future weaponry)
Includes bibliographical references and index.
ISBN 1-4042-0521-7 (library binding)
1. Command and control systems—Juvenile literature. 2. Command of troops—
Juvenile literature.
I. Title. II. Series.
UB212.M385 2006
355.3'3041—dc22

                                       2005013689

Manufactured in the United States of America

On the cover: A diagram showing the different elements of a battlefield command system.

CONTENTS

INTRODUCTION

For thousands of years, wars have been fought by people wielding physical weapons on the ground or at sea. As technology advanced, the way in which wars were fought also changed. Battles began to take place in the air. Instead of personally leading the way into battle, generals and other commanders began to coordinate huge forces from a distance. War became bigger, more deadly to civilians as well as to soldiers, and ever more complex.

Despite this increasing complexity, there are basic ideas about warfare that have not changed. Today, as it did a thousand years ago, waging war and carrying out a battle plan require that the general, admiral, or whoever is in charge has the following resources at his or her command:

WARFIGHTERS: These are men and women who serve in the military. They carry out the orders that result in battle, whether they are physically on the battlefield or operating from a distance.

WEAPONS: This could be anything from a gun to a missile. It might be something used directly (such as a soldier launching a grenade) or indirectly (such as the firing of a laser by a satellite).

INTELLIGENCE: This covers the entire field of gathering and evaluating information about the terrain, the enemy forces, the enemy's weapons, the weather, and everything else the commander might need to know before and during battle. On a larger scale, it should also include everything that will be important in the aftermath of a battle. Without adequate intelligence ahead of time, one might win a battle then lose what was gained by not being prepared for the dangers or obstacles that remain after the battle.

COMMUNICATION: It is vital to have open and reliable lines of communication between the commanders, the warfighters, and all elements involved in the battle. This communication must be two-way—information must be able to pass from command to the battlefield and from the battlefield to command. It's also important to be able to receive outside communication that could affect the battle, such as a message from the enemy offering to surrender or a vital weather report that could affect the outcome of the battle.

These four resources are tied together by what is known as a battlefield command system. In many ways, the battlefield command system is like the brain of the military. A battlefield command system organizes all the information available, processes it, and then distributes it to whoever needs it most. Success in warfare begins with a well-organized and technologically advanced battlefield command system. In this book, we'll examine battlefield command systems and the ways in which they contribute to the changing nature of warfare.

UNDERSTANDING THE BATTLEFIELD

Before one can explore the complexity of future battlefield command systems, it's necessary to understand how the very concept and definition of "battlefield" has changed over the thousands of years in which war has been waged.

In the most ancient days of war, a battlefield was literally a field or open space large enough for the opposing sides of warriors to face off, charge, and attack one another with swords, axes, slingshots, spears, or clubs. Battle grew more complex as new weapons were added, such as bows and chariots, and warriors began fighting from horseback.

THE FIRST DOMAIN OF WAR: LAND

A field of battle was seldom chosen at random. There was the advantage of those who lived on the land and knew it and were defending their own turf. An invader had to use

This painting depicts the relaying of orders during the siege of Yorktown in 1781. The man pointing in the center is General Rochambeau of France. Standing to his left is the future president of the United States George Washington. During this era, commanders were stationed close to the battlefield so that their orders could be delivered quickly to the front by men on foot or horseback.

scouts to learn about the land and find a place to fight that would provide an advantage.

Those advantages might include choosing a field that is bordered by a swamp to prevent the enemy from an easy escape or to make it impossible for the enemy to use chariots. It might involve finding a field with a hill on which to take the upper ground, forcing the enemy to expend energy charging up the hill. It might involve arranging warriors so the morning sun would be at their backs, forcing the enemy to fight with the sun in their eyes. It might involve hiding parts of your forces until the battle is under way, then signaling for them to attack, creating chaos and confusion among the ranks of the enemy.

GIVING ORDERS

Throughout history, winning battles and taking control of enemy territory has required the use of reliable battlefield command systems. In the beginning, that system might have been as simple as bellowing orders (hoping your voice could be heard above the clashing of swords and shields) or sending a runner or rider to deliver messages to another part of your forces.

Another way to communicate on the battlefield was through the use of horns, cymbals, drums, or other sound-making devices to send signals. Battlefield command was also aided by banners, standards, insignia, coats of arms, helmet decorations, and other visual devices to identify who was who in the general confusion of the battle.

THE SECOND DOMAIN OF WAR: WATER

When battles expanded beyond land, the second domain of war became water. Warriors would build ships to carry them on raids or into battle. As on land, visual devices such as flags, banners, and insignia were used to identify who was a friend or a foe. Drums, pipes, horns, and other means of making sound that could be heard across an entire ship were used to send signals.

THE THIRD DOMAIN OF WAR: AIR

The next domain of war that appeared was the air. Land and sea forces were joined by planes and balloons. Wars became larger. The battlefield covered more territory, sometimes involving

THREE USEFUL MILITARY TERMS

Strategy: The branch of military science dealing with command and the planning and conduct of a war. This is the big view of how an entire war should be fought and won.

Tactics: The branch of military science dealing with detailed maneuvers to achieve objectives set by strategy. This means the more specific actions that are taken to win a particular battle or section of a battle.

Logistics: The aspect of military operations that deals with getting all the people, transportation, weapons, ammunition, and food to the battlefront, and then replenishing the people and supplies as needed.

entire countries. Airplanes could not only fight other airplanes but could also drop bombs and bring back vital information about the enemy.

WORLD WAR I (1914–1918)

Air warfare became significant in World War I, but battlefield command systems remained limited. There were telegraphs or men in vehicles or on horses carrying messages, but initially there was no way to communicate with a pilot in a biplane as he set out to fight the enemy. This was also the war that introduced submarine warfare and the use of hideous new weapons, such as poison gas.

The revolutionary form of quick battlefield communication adopted for World War I was radio, also called wireless. At first, it could only transmit codes, such as Morse code. Later, it was able to transmit voices. The United States promptly took over all radio technology for the war, shutting down any civilian use of radio transmitters for fear of radio being used for espionage.

Both sides in the war made critical use of radio to communicate with men in the trenches, ships at sea, and airplanes or zeppelins. For the first time, there was a quick way for the war planners to send and receive information from various battlefields during the course of battle. They were able to react more quickly to changing situations in the field, to organize air squadrons that acted as units rather than individuals, and to reach ships at sea with new orders or information. It was also important for logistics. With the war being fought on so many fronts, there were new challenges in moving men, weapons, ammunition, and supplies to where they were needed.

World War I also marked the use of new strategies of deception. The French transmitted phony command signals to the German zeppelins, providing them with false navigational directions. Instead of flying safely home, the zeppelins flew over antiaircraft guns that shot them down. In World War I, the ability to destroy or subvert the enemy's communications became a vital part of battlefield command.

A sailor operates a radio transmitter in 1919. During World War I, radio increased the range and complexity of battlefield command systems. Radio allowed commanders to communicate over long distances and receive information faster than ever before. Radio technology also created a new type of spy who was responsible for intercepting and decoding the enemy's radio transmissions.

WORLD WAR II (1939–1945)

For World War II, the revolution in battlefield command systems continued as radio became more powerful and refined, telephone and cable technology grew, and technology such as radar (to detect the enemy in the air) and sonar (to detect the enemy underwater) were developed. The sheer number of armies, ships, submarines, and airplanes required bigger and better battlefield command systems. Technology had advanced, but there was still much room for improvement. Radio, for example, had limitations in power and distance, and it only allowed the use of voice or the transmission of codes.

THE FOURTH DOMAIN OF WAR: SPACE

Then the fourth domain of war was born—space. It's hard in this day and age to imagine the kind of shock Americans experienced when the Russians lofted the first satellite, *Sputnik*, into orbit in 1957. There was almost panic, as Americans imagined Russians dropping nuclear bombs on them from space. This led to the establishment of NASA (National Aeronautics and Space Administration) and a race to improve rockets and get more technology into space.

This spawned perhaps the most important giant step in battlefield command systems—satellite communications. The first limited communication satellite, *Echo 1*, was sent aloft by the United States in 1960. Also in 1960, the United States launched *Tiros 1*, the first weather satellite, and the navy put up a navigation satellite called *Transit 1B*. *Telstar*, launched in 1962, could transmit television signals.

The military was able to use satellites to take photos of nearly any location on Earth and to direct TV, radio, and telephone signals over vast distances. Satellite transmissions were far quicker and more powerful than land-based radio or any other form of communication available at the time.

GPS (global positioning system) is another advancement as a result of satellite technology. Someone with a GPS device can determine his or her specific location anywhere on the planet. GPS has become vital to military planning and operations.

A global positioning system satellite is pictured high above Earth. The global positioning system consists of twenty-four satellites operated by the United States Department of Defense. The first GPS satellite was launched in 1978, and the system became fully operational in 1993. Many weapons today, such as "smart bombs," are guided by GPS satellites.

THE FIFTH DOMAIN OF WAR: CYBERSPACE

Finally, along came the computer. The computer has created the fifth domain of modern warfare—cyberspace. It has also created a new form of war, known as information warfare. Information warfare is being fought with computer hardware, software, satellites, and fiber-optic networks. This type of warfare doesn't use conventional weapons. Instead, hackers use computer worms and viruses as weapons. Today, the U.S. military is actively developing technologies to compete in this new domain of war. In the future, the focus on war in cyberspace will only increase.

The Hacked NetDex.Inc

Complete Internet Services

This Page Has Been Hacked By Analyzer
I hacked this page in order to make things right
Makaveli did NOT hacked any of those DOD systems
he dont even know how to trojan a system
if u searching anyone u should search for me.

In 1998, a teenager from Israel named Ehud Tenenbaum and two teenagers from California hacked into over 400 United States military Web sites. Above is a screen shot of a Web site hacked by Tenenbaum, who called himself "Analyzer." The attacks, known as Solar Sunrise, exposed a major security hole in the U.S. military cybernetwork.

THE REACH OF BATTLEFIELD COMMAND SYSTEMS

Current and future battlefield command systems must quickly and efficiently reach across the entire globe, all the oceans and seas, and throughout air and space. In addition, they must reach into the realm of the computer, where communications and information and processing of data combine to create a virtual battlefield, or, as some call it now, a battlespace.

THE REVOLUTION IN MILITARY AFFAIRS

In military circles, the attempt to transform a twentieth-century American military into a high-tech military of the future is known as a revolution in military affairs (RMA). There have been other RMAs in the past, but the current RMA is about transforming an older military system into a new and improved military system designed to deal with enormous changes in how, why, when, and where battles will be fought.

The military is being asked to take on roles that it hasn't traditionally handled in the past, such as counterterrorism activities, hostage rescues, peacekeeping operations using nonlethal weapons, disaster relief, and trying to stop the illegal drug trade.

Another concern is the pace of technology development. In the civilian world, technology is improved and upgraded at an increasingly faster pace. In the past, when the entire world operated at a slower pace, the military could devote ten or fifteen years to develop a new weapon, a new tank, or a new plane. Given the pace of the modern world, the military recognizes the need to develop and incorporate new technology in months rather than years. It is also necessary to be able to respond to quickly changing world situations, crises, and developments at a speed that can keep up with the emerging threats.

ASYMMETRIC WARFARE

The most pressing of the threats driving the RMA is asymmetric warfare. In the twentieth century, war was fought between nations using official military forces. These are forces authorized by the government to fight for their country, and they are trained and paid by the government for that purpose. They operate under an established chain of command, wear specific uniforms, and use the specific type of gear and weapons designated for war.

Even in war there are rules, and civilized nations signed treaties and agreements on such issues as the fair treatment of enemy combatants, the designation of appropriate targets during war, and the banning of nuclear, chemical, and biological weapons. This was traditional warfare in which army A would face off with army B on a field of battle.

The world has shifted away from this type of warfare. Today, warfare is often characterized by regional conflicts carried out by rebels, warlords, or other nonofficial leaders. Threats from rogue powers (such as North Korea) and terrorist or guerrilla attacks have also changed the nature of warfare.

The attacks on the World Trade Center in New York City on September 11, 2001, are an example of asymmetric warfare. In the future, the U.S. military predicts that wars will tend to be of the asymmetric type. Because of this, the military is transforming its weaponry and the way it is organized.

Asymmetric warfare refers to a smaller, weaker enemy being able to do damage to a larger, stronger force. Another version of this is known as fourth generation warfare (4GW), and it refers to any other way of confronting superior military forces without fighting on a standard battlefield where the superior forces are generally expected to win. An example of 4GW would be an enemy who knows it can't win against state-of-the-art jet aircraft, so it poisons the food that the pilots eat instead. Without pilots, the jet fighters are useless.

When terrorists flew commercial airliners into the World Trade Center towers and the Pentagon on September 11, 2001, they pulled off the most damaging asymmetric attack the world has seen to date.

DEALING WITH ASYMMETRIC THREATS

It's difficult for any standard military organization that is geared toward the traditional warfare of the past to deal with an asymmetric threat. The terrorists don't represent an entire country, so there is no clear, straightforward territory to attack in return. They don't fight using standard weapons and often resort to the lowest of low-tech means to achieve their ends. These low-tech weapons used by terrorists, such as car bombs, roadside bombs, and booby traps can be extremely difficult to protect against.

Terrorists hide and mingle with civilian populations, and they use civilians as shields. Sometimes they have the support of a portion of a civilian population that is willing to hide and feed them. They don't wear uniforms to declare who they are, and they operate in secrecy. They don't adhere to rules and they don't sign treaties, which means they will use any form of NBC (nuclear, biological, chemical) weapon they can obtain.

That's what keeps military and security experts up at night working out how to transform a traditional war-based military force into something that can deal effectively with asymmetric warfare.

ELEMENTS OF THE TRANSFORMATION

Restructuring the overall military requires dramatic changes in battlefield command systems. Three of the major elements in this restructuring are:

) Joint operations and interoperability

) Commercial off-the-shelf technology (COTS)

) Capabilities-based systems

There are four branches, or "services," of the U.S. military: army, navy, air force, and marines. There is also the coast guard, which is primarily meant for guarding the domestic shorelines but which can be called into duty when needed as a fifth branch of the military. Space operations are handled by the air force.

In the past, there have been many tensions between the different branches of the military. Each branch was in competition with the other. This meant there was a tendency for each of the services to develop its own unique control systems, technology, and communications.

For example, even today the services don't use the same method to determine how to target bombs, missiles, and artillery. The army defines the position of the target using grid squares. The air force uses degrees and decimals of degrees to complete the same task, while the navy uses degrees, minutes, and seconds.

JOINT OPERATIONS AND INTEROPERABILITY

Joint operations refer to the interaction of the four services, where each branch is dependent on the others to handle some part of the battle or operation. In Afghanistan from 2001 to 2002, Army Special Forces on the ground called in air strikes from the navy, and navy aircraft were refueled by air force tankers. This is the way of the future, where the four services must work seamlessly together, each relying on the other at an instant's notice.

This raises the issue of interoperability. Imagine you're with four friends and you have four different video-game machines. Someone gives you four copies of a game that can only be played by your type of machine. Suddenly, you have three machines that are useless because they don't have interoperability. In other words, they don't have the ability to operate together or read another machine's software. Your three friends can't take part in what you're doing.

This is a huge problem when it comes to creating battle plans that must be carried out with precision timing and reliable communications using all four services. They must be able to communicate with one another at the correct frequencies, share vital information, and adapt instantly if something goes wrong with the battle plan. Interoperability ensures that any branch of the military can mesh its technology, communications, and operations with any other branch.

And that doesn't begin to address joint operations with foreign allies. In these types of operations, the foreign ally has its own unique systems, controls, and weapons. The ally may even speak an entirely different language. Achieving interoperability with allies will be difficult, but it is important to future battle operations.

DEEPWATER

The service with the most advanced form of battlefield command systems currently in development is the U.S. Coast Guard. Its system is known as the Deepwater program. Deepwater will create complete interoperability between all assets of the coast guard, including ships on the water, bases on the shore, and aircraft such as helicopters. In addition, it's designed to be interoperable with the other branches of the military, as well as civilian first-responders such as police and firefighters.

The National Security Cutter (NSC) is one of the projects of the coast guard's Deepwater program. The NSC will be the flagship of the coast guard's future fleet. The NSC and the other ships and aircraft being built as part of the Deepwater program will be linked together with state-of-the-art communication systems. The first NSC is expected to be completed in April 2007.

COTS

COTS is the military acronym for "commercial off-the-shelf" technology. These are products that were originally designed for nonmilitary use. Software (such as Linux or Windows), cell phones, GPS receivers, and laptops are all example of commercial off-the-shelf technologies.

In the past, the military would take years and years, and spend millions of dollars, to have every single military item designed and made especially for them. Previously, the advanced products made for the military would later find their way into civilian usage. Now it's just the opposite. Civilian development of technology has outpaced what the military can afford to match.

A major focus of the revolution in military affairs is the need to increase the speed of technological development, as well as bring down the cost. One of the best ways the military has found to do this is to find advanced technology that already exists and can be adapted for military use.

In the case of computer equipment, that means using the fast, light machines made for the commercial market but increasing the durability of the machines. A laptop must be incredibly rugged to survive the conditions of battle. Software must have increased security measures. A cell phone must be more rugged to survive in the field, plus have additional features to make the phone secure from hacking and able to overcome jamming. GPS devices must also be improved in this manner, especially since enemy jamming is one of the biggest problems with GPS.

Overall, using modified COTS products has revolutionized the military's ability to stay on the cutting edge of technology for a lower budget. This trend is sure to continue in the future.

CAPABILITIES-BASED SYSTEMS

In the past, a commander who was looking at his available forces would think in terms of numbers. Earlier wars depended on having more equipment, more weapons, and more men than the other side. Battles were often won by use of brute force.

Those days are gone. Instead of blanketing an enemy area with dozens of bombs to increase the chances of hitting the target, the twenty-first-century military uses one precision-guided bomb designed to take out a specific target and nothing else.

Today, and continuing into the future, the emphasis of military strategy is on how a potential enemy might attack us and how we can be prepared to deal with it. This requires a major shift in thinking. The military has to evaluate:

- Every type of threat that can happen on a global scale, anywhere on the planet

- Every type of mission (ranging from traditional battle to humanitarian missions such as air drops of food)

- Every possible type of attack (ranging from an attack on the homeland to a virus attack on the Internet) from any possible enemy (whether a rogue state or a single terrorist)

Once these variables have been evaluated, the military must design, build, and integrate whatever platforms, weapons, or systems are capable of dealing with the threat. This includes

In the future, the U.S. military will continue to embark on humanitarian missions, including air drops of food and supplies to civilians in need. In the photograph above, crew members of a C-17A Globemaster III cargo aircraft prepare for an air drop over northern Afghanistan. The mission was part of the United States' military campaign known as Operation Enduring Freedom.

having enough force to prevent the enemy from taking action, as well as reacting to attacks. It also includes the use of psychological tactics to trick the enemy into making mistakes or scare the enemy into giving up. Every branch of the service on land, on sea, in the air, and in space must contribute both offensive and defensive capabilities.

The battlefield command systems must make them all work together.

3

BATTLESPACE AWARENESS

The fundamental purpose of all battlefield command systems of the future will be to create battlespace awareness. According to the January 2004 Defense Industrial Base Capabilities Study on battlespace awareness, the main goal is for the U.S. military to "see, understand and act" faster than its enemies. The Department of Defense describes the major battlespace awareness activities as being:

- Observing and collecting information
- Evaluating the information collected
- Finding efficient ways to receive, store, and compare information, then making sure the necessary information gets to the people who need it most
- Simulating and forecasting (for example, receiving raw information from weather satellites, then using that data

to create a simulation of how the weather will affect conditions on the battlefield)

) Command and control of all war-fighting assets (including people, weapons, and platforms)

) Total connection between all decision makers through an information network

The idea behind battlespace awareness is that the top military decision makers will have a constant real-time source of information about any environment and any adversary that they may have to confront. The information will help them see an upcoming crisis and find a way to defuse it before it leads to battle, or help them deploy forces to deal with the problem as it occurs.

Then, while the forces are on the field dealing with the problem, the commanders will continue to receive real-time information from many sources, from satellites to the individual warfighter on the ground. These sources will continuously update what is happening in the battlespace. Commanders and decision makers are spread around the world, so it is vital to have an instant and reliable shared battlespace awareness. This is a network-centric approach.

THE GLOBAL INFORMATION GRID

Network-centric warfare covers the idea of having every warfighter, sensor, weapon, platform, and computer tied together by secure, high-broadband transmissions to

WHAT IS REAL TIME?

This means that information, communication, or other data are transmitted from the original source to a receiver without any delay. There is no lag in reaching the other end except for the time it takes for the data to travel through the communication lines (such as phone lines, cable lines, or satellite feeds). IM (instant messaging) is an example of real-time communication.

Real-time technology is a vital part of battlefield command and is increasingly becoming a part of everyday life. The Pioneer AVIC-N2 satellite navigation system is a commercially available device that provides near real-time traffic conditions.

create a battlespace network. This network will be part of a larger information system known as the Global Information Grid (GIG).

The GIG will be a super-Internet for use by the military, civilian contractors on military projects, and foreign allies. It will be as fast as technology allows, using fiber optics or satellite relays. It will use the newest and most powerful hardware and software.

The GIG will collect, assemble, and share billions of pieces of information from all over the world. The GIG will put this massive information together and present it in a form similar to Web pages, making it easy to access, understand, and update. The GIG will be accessible anywhere military personnel need to be, whether the location is permanent or in motion, or on the battlefield.

In addition to sharing information, the GIG will be used to coordinate logistics such as making travel arrangements, keeping track of stocks of ammunition, and handling payroll for military and civilian personnel. It will also be used to keep track of our forces and enemy forces, update weather reports, and provide maps and information about any possible battlefield.

THE OODA LOOP

The GIG will enable the battlefield commanders to vastly improve what is known as an OODA loop. OODA stands for "observe, orient, decide, act." It was popularized by visionary U.S. Air Force colonel John Boyd. Boyd studied warfare through the ages, especially the work of the ancient Chinese military writer Sun Tzu and found that more agile armies had defeated larger and more technologically advanced opponents on a frequent basis.

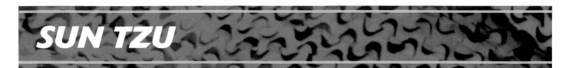

SUN TZU

Little is known about the warrior-philosopher Sun Tzu. It is thought he lived in eastern China somewhere between the sixth and third centuries BC. He is famous for writing *The Art of War*. His thoughts and ideas about warfare are so profound that he has been a major

source of study and inspiration for thousands of years. Even corporations have used his ideas to reshape their businesses.

One of his most famous quotes is: "If you know the enemy and know yourself, in a hundred battles you will never be in peril. When you are ignorant of the enemy but know yourself, your chances of winning and losing are equal. If ignorant both of your enemy and yourself, you are certain in every battle to be in peril."

Unfortunately, there are no known surviving portraits of Sun Tzu, the renowned Chinese military strategist and author of *The Art of War*. This is a traditional rendering of his appearance and style of dress.

Boyd concluded that the more agile competitor is able to observe, orient, decide, and act more quickly than his opponent. The OODA loop requires that a decision maker:

) Observe almost instantly what is happening in a battle

) Evaluate (orient) his observations about what is happening

) Use that orientation to make a split-second decision

) Act on the decision

After the decision maker acts, the loop begins again and repeats endlessly until the battle is over.

If the warfighter can do this quickly without being too obvious and with a certain amount of unpredictability, the opponent's OODA loop is disrupted. The opponent then becomes confused, indecisive, and more prone to panic or make mistakes.

The OODA loop is not just about physical quickness; it's mostly about mental quickness. The OODA loop applies to individual warfighters, such as a pilot, a sailor, or a land soldier, and it applies up the chain of command to the very top.

4

THE C4ISR SYSTEM OF SYSTEMS

"System of systems" refers to an approach of creating numerous smaller systems that function together as one larger unified system, with the various individual systems remaining flexible and easy to change.

A small-scale example of this would be a desktop computer. It consists of the computing system (CPU, motherboard, and memory chips), the input systems (keyboard and mouse), the processing systems (software), the visual system (monitor), the sound system (speakers), and peripheral systems (printer and scanner). It can have subsystems such as the hard drive, DVD drive, video card, or sound card. Any one of these systems or subsystems can be swapped out to upgrade the technology, and new systems or subsystems can be added as needed. Yet they all work

The command and control vehicle will be a mobile command center of the future army. It is part of a larger set of systems called the Future Combat Systems (FCS). In addition to the command and control vehicle, FCS will be made up of nineteen other systems. These systems include ground sensors, robots, and unmanned aerial vehicles. The Future Combat Systems are expected to be ready for use in 2014.

together as a system of systems to do whatever it is you need at the time.

The ultimate battle command system of systems is C4ISR, which stands for:

C4 = Command, control, communications, computers

I = Intelligence

S = Surveillance

R = Reconnaissance

C4: COMMAND, CONTROL, COMMUNICATIONS, COMPUTERS

C4 is the first component of the C4ISR system of systems. Providing complete command and control over the entire military is an unbelievably complex problem. Being able to send and receive secure communications that can't be hacked or jammed is a necessity. Computer networks have made such a system possible. In the future, the technology behind C4 will continue to be refined and improved.

THE TACTICAL INTERNET

An essential part of the C4 is called the tactical Internet. This is a wireless subsystem designed for a specific fighting force (such as an army platoon). Every truck, tank, plane, helicopter, drone, ship, or mobile platform that is a part of the tactical Internet will have a tracking device so it can be located anywhere on the planet. Each warfighter will have a GPS unit to get and give his or her position. Special vehicles carry transmission towers to enable the wireless network to work in remote areas and to connect to satellites.

Each of the platforms or warfighters in the fighting unit will have a computer screen with icons showing the positions of all the warfighters and the positions of enemy forces on full-color terrain maps. Friendly forces have blue icons. The enemy's forces, supplies, and minefields show as red icons. Clicking or touching the icons provides additional

This photo was taken on March 11, 2003, at the air operations center at Prince Sultan Air Base in Saudi Arabia during Operation Iraqi Freedom. Air operations centers direct air traffic, process surveillance information, and serve as control centers for unmanned aerial vehicles. In the future, the military is hoping to improve the speed at which information is received and processed at operations centers. Technology will also be improved to make this information available to commanders and soldiers from all four services.

A soldier models a prototype of a helmet that is planned to be part of the army's Land Warrior system. The helmet features a drop-down display that allows the soldier to view video, GPS data, or maps. The Land Warrior system will link soldiers to each other and allow them to connect to the tactical Internet. The army plans to begin testing the system, which also consists of body armor, a computer, and advanced weapons, in 2006.

information. A yellow diamond indicates a fallout zone in case of chemical or biological attacks.

The icons on the screen will be continuously updated from many sources, such as an advance team who spots a new enemy position and enters the data using its own special handheld device. Data are stored on removable cartridges so that warfighters can transport data from one vehicle to another if they are unable to transmit it. Information can also be sent as e-mail, if it is less urgent.

THE COMMAND POST OF THE FUTURE

Data from the tactical Internet will flow into the command post of the future (CPOF). The CPOF takes command and control into the field where mobile command centers are used to link together forces operating in the battlespace. Data comes through real-time feeds from satellites and from warfighters with video feeds, from robotic sensors, and from other sources coming through the tactical Internet. With this technology, the physical battlefield is constantly monitored.

Information is presented to each of the commanders involved in the operation using computers and monitors. They look at the same battlespace, at the same maps, photos, and video at the same time, and can communicate with one another about the shared "battleboard." Some commanders might be in remote locations near the battle, while others might be located on a navy ship or in a Pentagon office in the United States.

In return, they can relay additional information that the warfighters in the field might not have and can issue new orders as needed.

THE FOG OF WAR

The phrase "the fog of war" refers to how things can go wrong in battle due to chaos and confusion. At one time, it would have come from real fog on an ancient battlefield, which would keep the warriors from being able to tell friend from foe until

Army sergeant Christopher Gonzalez operates a computer inside a M1A1 Abrams main battle tank. Sergeant Gonzalez is stationed in Iraq as part of Operation Iraqi Freedom. The army is in the process of upgrading many of the Abrams tanks so that they will be able to link to command and control systems being developed, such as the command post of the future.

they were on top of one another, or from how a ship lost in fog could run aground and sink.

Confusion in a modern battle can lead to the terrible result of friendly fire, in which warfighters are mistakenly fired upon and killed by their own side. The CPOF shows where every warfighter is at every moment in the hope of preventing friendly fire from happening in the future.

THE FOG OF NETWORKS

The danger of relying on such highly networked systems is that a failure could lead to confusion or ineffectiveness on the battlefield. The C4 system has to anticipate problems such as the destruction of vital fiber-optic cables, computer virus attacks, jammed communications, or damaged satellites. The enemy could set off an electromagnetic pulse (EMP) bomb that could destroy all electronic equipment for miles.

Having a constant source of power to run networked systems is another problem when operating on a remote battlefield. There's also the possibility that an overworked system might simply crash (a common problem with any computer).

A single Abrams tank has fifty microprocessors and they all need to talk to one another in order for the tank to function. If something destroys their ability to communicate, the tank becomes a huge hunk of useless metal.

In an article appearing in *BusinessWeek*, Lieutenant Colonel Steven H. Mattos, director of the technology division at the Marine Corps Warfighting Laboratory in Quantico, Virginia, said, "If you put a hole in a paper map, you have a map with a hole in it. You put a bullet through a computer screen, what do you have? A piece of junk."

That's why warfighters must be trained in numerous ways to accomplish their missions, with or without the advanced technology.

INTELLIGENCE, SURVEILLANCE, AND RECONNAISSANCE

The "ISR" part of "C4ISR" consists of intelligence, surveillance, and reconnaissance.

Intelligence is information about an enemy or potential enemy that can be used for political or military advantage. For the military, intelligence is vital in planning operations and offensives. A large part of intelligence comes from spies, known as HUMINT (human intelligence). Other types of intelligence are IMINT (imagery intelligence) and ELINT (electronic intelligence).

Surveillance is the systematic observation of air, surface, or subsurface areas by visual, electronic, photographic, or other means, for intelligence or other purposes. Surveillance is ongoing and general, and may or may not be used in a military action. A satellite that routinely photographs the territory of a foreign nation is a form of surveillance.

Reconnaissance is a military mission undertaken to obtain information by visual observation or other detection methods about the activities and resources of an enemy or potential enemy. It can also be performed to learn more about the terrain of a particular area. Reconnaissance usually comes right before a military action and has a more specific purpose than surveillance.

UAVS AND UCAVS

A major change in conducting ISR on the battlefield is the use of robots and sensors. These technologies are valuable because they can gather dangerous information without risking human warfighters. One of the most important innovations in this field has been the development of unmanned aerial vehicles (UAVs) and unmanned combat aerial vehicles (UCAVs). UAVs and UCAVs are robotic drones that fly above the battlefield and over enemy terrain, often at a lower altitude than is safe for a manned aircraft.

A UAV carries video cameras, infrared cameras, and a whole range of sensors to gather information about the enemy's location and movements. The UAV transmits this information back through the tactical Internet or to the larger network-centric force via radio or satellite.

A UCAV can do the same things but with the addition of a weapons payload. For example, a commander can receive a visual report from the UCAV that shows an enemy about to fire a rocket toward his forces. The commander can immediately order the UCAV to fire a missile at that enemy. The UCAV

Pictured above is an artist's envisioning of an unmanned combat armed rotorcraft (UCAR). The UCAR is essentially a heavily armed, remote-controlled helicopter. A number of aircraft manufacturers are currently working on the project for the U.S. Army. The army hopes to have a version of the UCAR ready for action around 2012.

allows for a much faster response in the battlespace without having to send in troops who might be harmed.

The following are examples of UAVs and UCAVs already at work.

Predator (UAV/UCAV)

The Predator is 27 feet (8.2 meters) long with a wingspan of nearly 49 feet (15 m). It can cruise at 84 miles per hour (135 kilometers per hour) up to 25,000 feet (7,620 m) high and can stay in the air for 24 hours. A Predator is controlled by a crew who can be many thousands of miles away. It carries cameras, plus sensors that can detect heat rising from enemy troops, tanks, or missiles. Though initially designed for ISR, it has been adapted to carry Hellfire missiles, which can take out tanks, buildings, satellite dishes, and trucks. The Predator can also carry and drop mini-UAVs to carry out shorter, close-up missions. A new version of the Predator is being developed that will be larger and more deadly than the original.

Mini UAVs

Also called tactical UAVs, these are about the size of model airplanes. The marines call theirs the Dragon Eye. Micro-UAVs are being designed that are so tiny that an enemy will mistake them for insects.

Global Hawk (UAV)

The enormous Global Hawk operates very high up at 60,000 feet (18,300 m). It can transmit close-up images of the ground in any weather condition to a base thousands of miles away. It's 44 feet (13.4 m) long with a wingspan of 116 feet (35.4 m). It can fly for long distances and remain in the air for 30 to 40 hours. Future Global Hawks will be even bigger.

ScanEagle (UAV)

The ScanEagle is 4 feet (1.2 m) long with a wingspan of 10 feet (3 m). It can remain in the air up to 15 hours (future models will be able to fly for 30 hours) and can fly up to 16,000 feet (4,900 m).

The ScanEagle was successfully used to avoid friendly fire casualties during an assault on Fallujah during the second Iraq

The ScanEagle is a relatively inexpensive UAV developed by the Boeing Corporation. The ScanEagle is launched from a catapult, which can be seen in the above photograph. The ScanEagle does not require a human to guide it during flight. Instead, the UAV is preprogrammed to use the global positioning system to reach its destination.

war. The battle involved 10,000 soldiers and dozens of warplanes. ScanEagle continuously circled the city and transmitted vital data to the U.S. forces.

Boeing X-45 (UCAV)

The X-45 can travel about 495 miles per hour (797 km/h) at 35,000 feet (10,700 m). Its body is 26.5 feet (8 m) long and the wingspan is nearly 34 feet (10.4 m). It can drop a variety of satellite-guided bombs. It has a stealth configuration to help it escape detection and can deliver bombs more quickly than the slower Predator UCAVs. The X-45 is still being tested for future deployment on the battlefield.

In this photograph, an X-45 prototype releases a guided bomb during a test near China Lake, California. In the test, which occurred on April 18, 2004, the 250-pound (113 kg) bomb successfully struck its target. A future version of the aircraft, known as the X-45C, will be larger than the prototype and able to carry eight precision-guided bombs.

SWORDS ROBOT

In addition to the UAVs and UCAVs, other technologies are in development to aid military surveillance and reconnaissance. SWORDS, or special weapons observation reconnaissance detection systems, are heavy-duty battle robots that are about 3 feet (1 m) high and move on two treads. They're run by a remote operator who sees through the robot's video cameras, which include night vision and zoom lenses. The SWORDS robot is heavily armed with automatic weapons and has extreme targeting accuracy to take out enemies. Its cameras and sensors send information back through the tactical Internet.

Design engineer Gary Morin demonstrates the SWORDS robot in this photograph taken on January 14, 2005. The robot is manufactured by Foster-Miller, a company based out of Massachusetts. The SWORDS robot is expected to be the first armed robotic vehicle to be used in combat. It is designed to be especially useful in urban combat operations.

SENSORS

Sensors of all types will play an important role in adding to the capabilities of C4ISR. Extremely tiny sensors called Smart Dust have been developed that can be spread by the hundreds or thousands over a wide area. They are networked together to relay information while being nearly invisible. Current Smart Dust sensors are about the size of a wristwatch, but advances in miniaturization may bring them down to the size of a grain of sand. They might even become small enough to float in the air like dust.

These sensors could be used to detect chemical and biological agents, motor exhaust, human odors, or vibrations caused by large vehicles nearby. They could also use acoustic abilities to listen for sounds in the ground in order to find hidden underground structures.

MICROSATELLITES

Today, hundreds of satellites are in orbit around Earth. They serve a number of different purposes, including communications, weather monitoring, scientific analysis, television broadcasting, and espionage. There are military spy satellites that can read a newspaper from their positions 200 to 400 miles (320 to 640 km) above Earth.

For future battlefield command systems, a set of a dozen or more microsatellites weighing less than 1,000 pounds (450 kilograms) each, or nanosatellites weighing less than 40 pounds (18 kg) each will be orbited using smaller, expendable rockets launched from beneath the wings of aircraft. These networked satellites will be able to concentrate their cameras and sensors on specific battlefield areas.

INFORMATION WARFARE

Along with war that is fought on land, on sea, in the air, and in space, there is the fifth domain of war in cyberspace, commonly referred to as information warfare (IW). The United States is especially dedicated to achieving information superiority in order to win on real battlefields and in virtual battlefields.

The primary virtual battlefield of IW is the civilian Internet. In this way of thinking, the entire Internet is a type of battlefield command system in which the information it contains can be a defense, a weapon, or a tool. It is also something that absolutely must be defended from attack by hackers and cyberwarriors.

CRITICAL INFRASTRUCTURE

Nearly every corner of the world is linked to the Internet through the use of hundreds of millions of computers. The reach of the Internet is enormous and continuously growing. In the United States, the Internet and networked computers connected to the Internet have become integrated into the national critical infrastructure. This means that the nation's internal systems that make things run or function require the Internet to work properly.

Critical infrastructure includes controlling satellites, power grids, railroads, air traffic, traffic signals, subways, and water systems. It also affects communications, banking, investing, inventory, shipping, and the operation of businesses of all kinds. There are even surgeries being performed remotely over the Internet, with the patient in one city and the surgeon in another.

Imagine the disruption that a terrorist hacker could cause if he or she were to cut off the power system, microwave towers, traffic signals, and phones in a major city. It would effectively shut down the city completely. People would be trapped in traffic, subways, or trains and would be unable to use land phones or cell phones. Add a coordinated terrorist attack with a biological or chemical weapon to this scenario, and it's a recipe for a major disaster.

THE INTERNET UNDER ATTACK

By now, everyone is familiar with security problems on computers caused by hackers sending out viruses and worms via e-mail. In 2003, the estimated damage from the Blaster worm alone was $525 million.

The Department of Homeland Security has formed the National Cyber Security Division (NCSD) for the purpose of finding weaknesses in the Internet and fixing them. It deals with incidents affecting federal, state, local, private sector, and international partners.

However, military computers are also connected to the Internet. There have been some famous attacks on military computer systems by this method. In a 1998 incident called Solar Sunrise, computer systems at air force and navy bases were attacked by two teenage hackers in California and a third teenager in Israel. Another significant security breach of air force computers was caused by a sixteen-year-old boy in north London, while in another incident the navy and NASA were hacked by a twenty-one-year-old man in Argentina. These young hackers were doing it for the fun and challenge, but what if they had been terrorists?

PROTECT, DETECT, REACT

It's well known that terrorist and criminal groups use the Internet to spread their propaganda, recruit new members, coordinate attacks, and pass along secret information. Therefore, a significant part of IW is finding ways to disrupt those activities. The IW "weapons" being developed include biological microorganisms that can eat, burn, or disable the hardware in enemy computers. Software viruses are also being developed that can destroy the information and operating systems on those computers.

SERIOUS GAMES

Warfighters who grow up playing video games find it easy to adjust to a gamelike interface such as the tactical Internet. This reality has led to the development of "serious games." The idea behind serious games is to have game developers use their advanced visual and design skills to create game-based simulations for non-entertainment purposes.

This can include subjects such as health care, university management, peacekeeping, hazardous chemical cleanup, and battlefield situations. Two serious games have been created for the army: a training program called *Full Spectrum Warrior* and the online simulation *America's Army*.

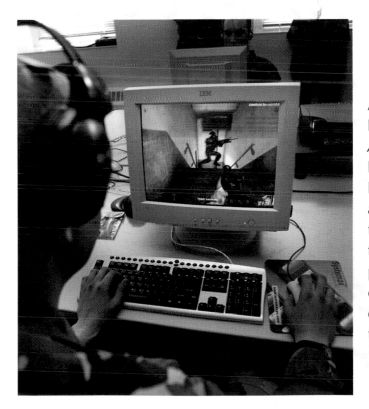

Army specialist David Hesson plays the *America's Army* video game at Fort Lewis in Washington. Hesson was participating in a competition between a team of four soldiers and a team of four civilian game players. The civilians defeated the soldiers in four out of the five matches contested.

In turn, the U.S. military must defend civilian use of the Internet as well as the security of military computers and the Global Information Grid. This defensive stance is known as Protect, Detect, React.

AIR FORCE INFORMATION WARFARE CENTER

Much of the work on Protect, Detect, React is being done at the Air Force Information Warfare Center (AFIWC) at the Lackland Air Force Base in Texas. At the base, more than 1,000 military and civilian experts focus on ways to protect computer systems and networks, detect intruders, and come up with ways to react to intrusions, as well as many other areas of research.

Some of the IW weapons and technologies that have been developed or are in development at the base include:

- IDS (intrusion detection systems), which are automated programs specifically designed to monitor computer systems against hacking attempts

- ASIM (automated security incident measurement), which is both hardware and software that sits on air force networks listening for suspicious intruders

- Coordinated Noise and Aimpoint, which are extremely secretive projects dealing with the use of directed energy weapons, such as microwaves or lasers, to strike with precision at enemy information systems

Another important IW program at the AFIWC is called Sensor Harvest. This is a tool that analyzes information in order to determine the best way to defend against, deceive, or attack enemy forces. The teams of analysts gather everything they can find about a potential enemy's military capability, weapons, economy, culture, geography, politics, and information systems. The data is analyzed to find the critical areas of leadership, military force, infrastructure, and physical facilities. The information is then used to develop an appropriate strategy.

INFORMATION AS A WEAPON

One of the big shifts in thinking about IW is that information itself can be a weapon. Information can be used to promote dangerous ideas and beliefs, or to spread beneficial ideas and beliefs. It can be used to generate fear or to dispel fear. Spreading false information can mislead the enemy into making mistakes. Blocking information can stop an enemy from being able to fight back.

In the future of IW, those who control information will control the war.

BATTLEFIELD COMMAND SYSTEMS OF THE TWENTY-FIRST CENTURY

The battlefield command systems of the future strive to make the future warfighter and fighting forces flexible, agile, quick, and lethal. These systems will provide almost instant information from sources across the globe and in the distant reaches of

Major Michael Mras views a computer monitor showing the ground movement of enemy troops. Major Mras is a sensor management officer in the U.S. Air Force 116th Air Control Wing. A major aim of battlefield command in the future will be to decrease the time it takes to relay pertinent information concerning the enemy to forces on the ground, in the air, and at sea.

space. The weapons they command will become more precise in an attempt to reduce civilian casualties. The robots and sensors under their control will save the lives of many warfighters in the field.

It's entirely possible that future wars will be fought in cyberspace instead of in the "real world," where damage to the Internet and connected infrastructure can be as devastating as a traditional land battle.

In 1967, the original *Star Trek* series aired an episode called "A Taste of Armageddon." In this episode, two planets had been at war for 500 years but were fighting a simulated war using only computers. When one side scored a hit, all the citizens in the affected area had to willingly report to disintegration chambers to be vaporized in order to maintain the balance of the virtual war. Captain Kirk destroys the computers, forcing the worlds to either make peace or face the terrible reality of true war.

As battlefield command systems become more and more like video games, it's vitally important that everyone involved, from the top commanders to the warfighters in planes, on the ground, or on ships, remember that the blips on their screens are not merely electronic icons. They represent flesh and blood people. The digital battlespace must never disguise the truth that war is a bloody, brutal activity undertaken only at great need.

Combat and killing will not be overcome with high-tech battle gear but with less deadly means. These means include diplomacy, an increased understanding of other cultures, increased global trade, and the fair distribution of diminishing resources such as water, food, land, and energy. To achieve peace, it is important to attack the causes of war instead of simply attacking the enemy with powerful weaponry.

As Sun Tzu wrote thousands of years ago, "Those who win every battle are not really skillful—those who render others' armies helpless without fighting are the best of all."

GLOSSARY

acronym A word formed usually from the first letters of a name, as in USA standing for United States of America.

coat of arms A visual design used on a shield to identify a particular warrior.

computer virus A computer program that is designed to replicate itself by copying itself into the other programs stored in a computer.

computer worm A malicious computer program that replicates itself until it fills all of the storage space on a drive or network.

CPU Central processing unit; the part of a computer that interprets and carries out instructions.

cyberspace The virtual world made up of computers connected to the Internet.

front An area of conflict between two armies.

infrastructure The underlying foundation of a system or organization.

insignia A badge used to identify someone's rank or official position.

microprocessor An entire CPU put onto a single computer chip.

Morse code A code consisting of dots and dashes that represent the letters of the alphabet.

payload The items carried by an aircraft.

platform Any mobile vehicle or base that is used to deliver weapons or resources to the battle. Tanks, Humvees, planes, ships, submarines, and satellites are examples of platforms.

propaganda The spread of information to advance the beliefs of a group or organization.

rogue state A nation that disregards international law and doesn't follow international standards of acceptable behavior.

sensor Any device that receives a signal or stimulus (such as heat, pressure, light, or motion) and responds to it in a distinctive manner.

zeppelin A large airship with a rigid structure that floats by means of gas bags filled with helium or hydrogen.

FOR MORE INFORMATION

Air Force Information Warfare Center
San Antonio, TX 78243
(210) 977-3549
Web site: http://afiwcweb.lackland.af.mil/home/index.cfm

United States Computer Emergency Readiness Team
Mail Stop 8500
245 Murray Lane SW
Building 410
Washington, DC 20528
(703) 235-5110
Web site: http://www.us-cert.gov

Marine Corps Warfighting Laboratory
3255 Meyers Avenue
Quantico, VA 22134
(703) 784-5096
Web site: http://www.mcwl.quantico.usmc.mil

Web Sites

Due to the changing nature of Internet links, the Rosen Publishing Group, Inc., has developed an online list of Web sites related to the subject of this book. This site is updated regularly. Please use this link to access the list:

http://www.rosenlinks.com/lfw/bcsf

FOR FURTHER READING

Alexander, John B. *Winning the War: Advanced Weapons, Strategies, and Concepts for the Post 9-11 World*. New York, NY: St. Martin's, 2003.

Coram, Robert. *Boyd: The Fighter Pilot Who Changed the Art of War*. New York, NY: Little, Brown, 2002.

Hammon, Grant T. *The Mind of War: John Boyd and American Security*. Washington, DC: Smithsonian Books, 2004.

Libicki, Martin C. *What Is Information Warfare?* Washington, DC: United States Government Printing Office, 1995.

Sun Tzu. *The Art of War*. Translated by Gary Gagliardi. Seattle, WA. Clearbridge Publishing, 2003.

Toffler, Alvin, and Heidi Toffler. *War and Anti-War: Survival at the Dawn of the 21st Century*. New York, NY: Warner Books, 1995.

Vizard, Frank, and Phil Scott. *21st Century Soldier: The Weaponry, Gear, and Technology of the Military in the New Century*. New York, NY: Popular Science, 2002.

BIBLIOGRAPHY

Adams, James. *The Next World War: Computers Are the Weapons and the Front Line Is Everywhere.* New York, NY: Simon & Schuster, 2001.

Air Force Information Warfare Center. "Current Missions." Retrieved March 11, 2005 (http://www.6901st.org/mission/ mission_reports.htm).

Anand, Vinod. "Future Battlespace and Need for Jointmanship." *Strategic Analysis*, Vol. 23, No. 10, Jan. 2000, pp. 1623–1640.

Bueno, Ricardo. "Global Information Grid—Questions and Answers." Retrieved March 11, 2005 (http://www. softwaretechnews.com/stn7-1/grid-qa.html).

Carey, John, Spencer E. Ante, Frederik Balfour, Laura Cohn, and Stan Crock. "Point, Click . . . Fire." *BusinessWeek*, April 7, 2003.

Deputy Under Secretary of Defense. "Defense Industrial Base Capabilities Study: Battlespace Awareness." 2004. Retrieved March 11, 2005 (http://www.acq.osd.mil/ip).

Deputy Under Secretary of Defense. "Defense Industrial Base Capabilities Study: Command and Control." 2004. Retrieved March 11, 2005 (http://www.acq.osd.mil/ip).

Deputy Under Secretary of Defense. "Transforming the Defense Industrial Base: A Roadmap." 2003. Retrieved March 11, 2005 (http://www.acq.osd.mil/ip).

Laird, Robbin F. "Transformation and the Defense Industrial Base: A New Model." 2003. Retrieved March 11, 2005 (http://www.ndu.edu/inss/DefHor/DH26/DH_26.htm).

Libicki, Martin C. *Illuminating Tomorrow's War.* Collingdale, PA: DIANE Publishing Company, 2000.

Richards, Chester W. *What If Sun Tzu and John Boyd Did a National Defense Review?* Washington, DC: Center for Defense Information, 2003.

Tiron, Roxana. "Computers in Combat: Double-Edged Swords." 2001. Retrieved March 11, 2005 (http://nationaldefense.ndia.org/issues/2001/Jun/Computers_in.htm).

INDEX

About the Author

Christy Marx is an author, researcher, and scriptwriter with over twenty-five years experience writing for many forms of media. Throughout her career, she has devoted special attention to researching and writing about varied topics in history, science, and technology, including military fiction. Her other science and technology books for Rosen Publishing include *Extreme Life in the Ocean Depths*, *Watson and Crick and DNA*, and the biography of navy admiral Grace Hopper, the first woman to program the first computer in the United States. For additional background, please visit http://www.christymarx.com.

Photo Credits

Cover courtesy of Rockwell Collins; cover (left corner) © Digital Vision/Getty Images; cover (top middle) © Photodisc Red/Getty Images; p. 7 and throughout U.S Marine Corps./Petty Officer 1st Class Ted Banks; p. 8 © The Art Archive/Musée du Château de Versailles/Dagli Orti; p. 12 © Bettmann/Corbis; p. 14 © AP/WideWorld Photos; p. 15 © AP/WideWorld Photos/HO/AntiOnline; p. 18 © age fotostock/Superstock; p. 22 © Integrated Coast Guard Systems; p. 25 U.S. Air Force photo by Tech. Sgt. Scott Reed; p. 28 © AP/WideWorld Photos/Richard Drew; p. 30 © The Bridgeman Art Library; p. 33 U.S Army; p. 35 © USAF/Royal Air Force Sgt. Gareth Davis/AP/WideWorld Photos; p. 36 © AP/WideWorld Photos/U.S. Army, HO; p. 38 DoD photo by Staff Sgt. Suzanne M. Day, U.S. Air Force; pp. 42, 44 © Boeing; p. 45 NASA/Jim Ross; p. 46 © AP/WideWorld Photos/Mike Derer; p. 51 © AP/WideWorld Photos/Ted S. Warren; p. 54 U.S. Air Force photo by Sue Sapp.

Designer: Evelyn Horovicz; Editor: Brian Belval